A HEAVEN FOR HORSES

Written by Pat Sheets

This Book Belongs To:

____

It is strange that the last book about Zip & Zoom would be was there a heaven for horses. I didn't know that in the near future they both would be deceased so soon.

As a horse lover and owner the pain of losing one of yours is indescribable. When you have put your heart and your soul in training a horse, they become a part of you. You spend hours and days teaching them the art of the trade.

Zip & Zoom both knew reining, sorting, barrels, poles and just riding in the river bottom for fun. Zip was very quick at turning, walking and running. She was beautiful palomino paint with a white mane and tail. I always gave her a bath before we went to shows. People thought she was so pretty they couldn't take their eyes off her. She loved for me to comb her pretty mane and tail and tell her she was pretty. Zip had to be doing something all of the time and had endless energy!

When I first got Zip, she was very thin and slim looking and I knew at first sight I had to have her. It didn't take long for her to put on weight and fill out. She was quite a handful at first; always having to buck when I would put the saddle on her. I would run her in the round pen until she quit bucking. If I said "reverse" she would immediately go the other way. Working cows came to her so easy as well as the barrels and poles.

One day as she was coming up to be fed, I noticed she had a limp in her left front leg. The next day the limp was in both front legs and had started on both back legs. Before long she could hardly walk and was in very bad pain. In my heart I knew she had grass-foundered. Tears began to come in my eyes for I knew it was bad. When this happens the boned in their feet drops and rotates. When it is so bad that you cannot reverse it, blood starts to seep around the hoof line and cause the hoof to come off. There is no cure to stop this.

I called the veterinarian and he agreed to ease her out of the terrible pain. We would have to put her to sleep. He would do this by giving her medicine to gradually slow her brain and heart until they stopped. I stood there holding her for the last time, crying endlessly; knowing it would be the last time. I held her face next to mine to tell her goodbye and how very much I loved her. I thanked her for the hours of enjoyment she had given me.

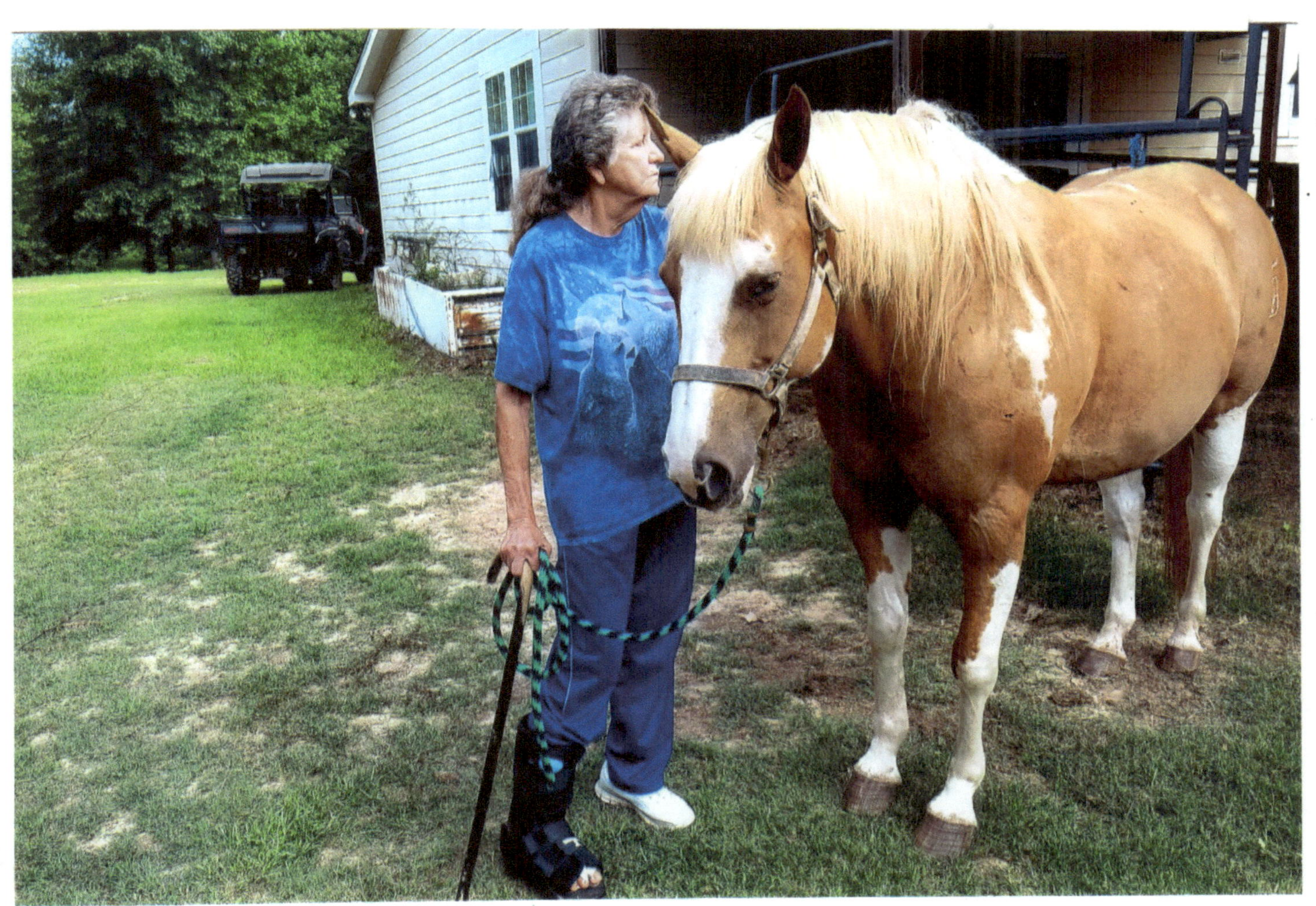

My son, Don and his wife Dana came over to help me out in this very sad time. Don had a backhoe to dig a gravesite for her. Dana held me while I cried. After the vet put her to sleep, Don carefully put her in the grave. He made sure she was placed where she would be comfortable. He said, "Mom, I wanted her to be perfect, just like she was asleep." I hugged him and thanked him for all he had done.

A month went by and I noticed Zoom had bowed a tendon. She loved to stand out in the pond to stay cool. She got very hot in the summer and very cold in the winter. She would paw the water and then dip her head under the water to stay cool. I think she got her back foot stuck in the mud which caused her tendon to bow. She could walk in it, but with a limp. She had limped on one of her front legs for about five years. My veterinarian, Rob tried different things to help her. I gave her bute every morning to ease the pain. Then later she came up with her right back leg hurt to the point she could not walk on it. I watched her for several days thinking maybe she would improve.

One morning, she was down and I could not get her up. I called Rob again and he said it was not good. He gave her a big pain shot and said if she doesn't get better by morning to call and he would have to put her down if that is what we wanted. She got up and made it to the barn, but she was in terrible pain. I knew I had no choice. Rob said he would be there at six o'clock. It was came a terrible storm. It was lightening and thundering and rain was coming down. I got her in a stable trying to comfort her. I loved on her and told her soon she would have no more pain and would rest peacefully. As Rob arrived, I loved on her while crying uncontrollably.

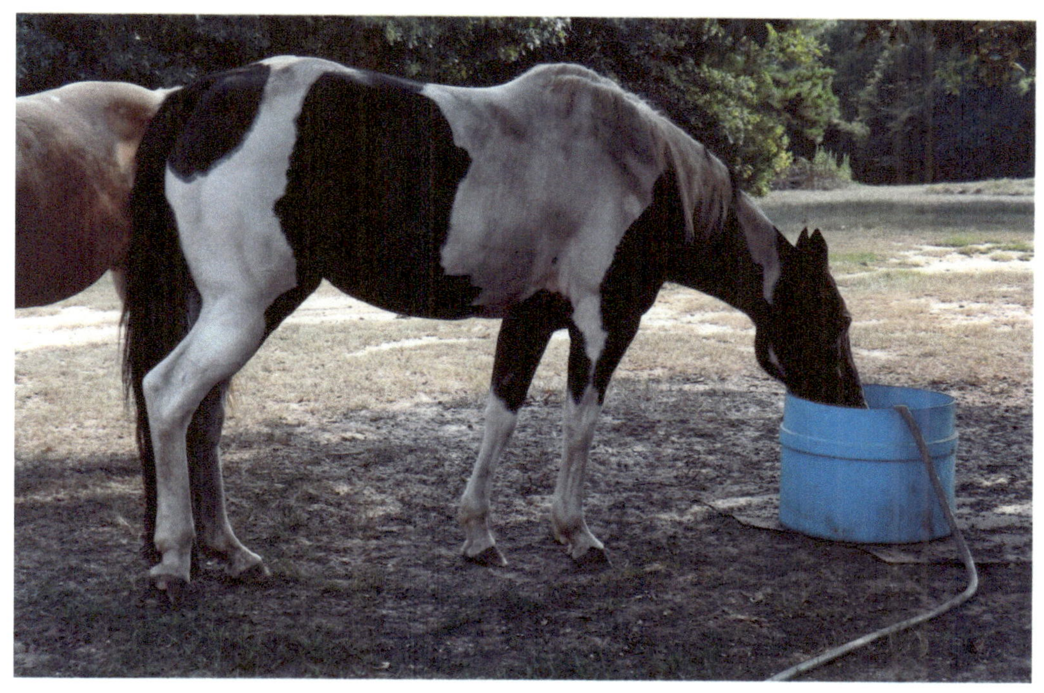

Thoughts came to me how much she had done for me. Zoom was a super cow horse and good running barrels and poles. She won numerous awards in team penning and sorting. She loved riding in the river bottom for pleasure. Three days before she became so crippled, I told Zoom, "let me give you a bath and make you pretty." She loved her bath and for me to comb her mane and tail. I think she thought maybe we were going to a team penning. I didn't know it would me my last time to bathe her. As I tied her in the sunshine to dry, she nuzzled me with her nose as if to say "let's go riding." I had to hug her and say, "not today, Zoom." There was no way she could carry me and the saddle on her back.

Kilgore Saddle Club
2006

Don came again, to dig her grave alongside Zip. Once again, he placed Zoom so carefully in the grave. He told me, "Mom, Zoom and Zip are side by side. They will be happy now they are close together." I held true to what I told them, that I would never part with them until the end.

I bet they are now running and playing without any pain and remembering all the good times we shared. Goodbye, Zip and Zoom and thanks again for all the pleasure you brought to me.

Love, Pat, Pat.

As days went by after they were gone, I still cried at times. I would look out at the pasture and I could see them standing close to each other eating grass. At times I wanted to call them up so they could be fed. Thank goodness for all the wonderful memories. They live on in my heart and mind. Bless you Zoom and Zip.

My husband, Dale was so sad about having to put Zoom and Zip down he also cried many times. When I say, "put down," let me explain. The vet gives them a shot in the main vein in their neck. This shot is medicine that stops their heart and lets them die peacefully. When animals have no more quality of life, then you make the decision to end it. For example, they cannot stand or lie down without being in tremendous pain. The pain being so bad they shake all over and their eyes show you they are begging for relief. It's the only humane thing you can do because you love them so and it ends their pain.

I can't thank my son, Don enough for the effort he put into burying Zoom and Zip so perfectly. He made sure they were placed so they would be comfortable. As he finished he gave me a big hug with tears in his eyes. I told him, "I love you, son, and thanks so much for all you have done."

(Zip and Zoom were the characters in the first three
books I wrote.)

*Thank you, God, for giving us horses.
They sure bring joy to our lives. - Pat Pat*

THE END

www.ingramcontent.com/pod-product-compliance
Lightning Source LLC
Chambersburg PA
CBHW042134030726
47599CB00002B/466